Ask...

(Life's Most Important Answers Are Found
in Asking the Right Questions)

John L. Mason

Unless otherwise indicated, all Scripture quotations are taken from the *King James Version* of the Bible.

1st Printing
10,000 Copies in Print

Ask... *(Life's Most Important Answers Are Found in Asking the Right Questions)*
ISBN 1-88810-307-8
Copyright © 1996 by John Mason
P.O. BOX 54996
Tulsa, OK 74155

Dedication

I am proud to dedicate this book to my beautiful wife, Linda, and our four great kids Michelle, Greg, Mike and Dave.

To Linda, for being my very best friend.
To Michelle "Moosh", for your love.
To Greg "The Z", for your non-stop sense of humor.
To Mike "Mister Mikey", for your inquisitiveness.
To Dave "The Kumba Man", for your contagious smile.

Introduction

Over the past several years, I have had the privilege of knowing and working with many successful people from various walks of life. As I observed these people, I noticed that the "success traits" each possessed varied greatly from one individual to another. For example, some were very organized, whereas others seemed only to "file by pile." And although some worked long hours, weekends, and holidays — many could have written the book *How To Work a Four-Hour Day*!

One thing I learned for sure: There are a lot of ways to succeed. However, one common characteristic that is usually overlooked really stood out to me about these successful people: They all had the ability to ask good questions. In fact, many asked great questions on a regular basis.

I saw that whether or not these people who had attained success took action was greatly influenced by the questions they asked. I also observed that as they asked more outstanding questions, their focus in life changed and improved. They automatically became more productive! I began to realize that quality questions = a quality life.

The Bible says, "Ask and you will receive" (Matt. 7:7) and "You have not because you ask not" (James 4:2). There is only one way to ask, and that is to pose a question! The way to receive is to ask questions.

That is why I wrote this book. I have collected a host of powerful questions that have impacted my life and the lives of others. These thought-provoking questions helped us find some of life's most important answers. I know they will do the same for you.

Remember, it's not only the questions you ask, but the questions you fail to ask, that shape your destiny. As you read this book, open your heart and mind. Let God whisper in your ear. Take action on the answers that come your way. Tap into the power of asking the right questions!

Looking
Inward

1

Do you need a good swift kick in the seat of your "can'ts"?

2

Do you count your blessings, or do you think your blessings don't count?

What good is aim if you never pull the trigger?

Napoleon is quoted as saying: "'Impossible' is a word found only in the dictionary of fools." What words are found in *your* dictionary?

Are you willing to fight for your dream? (You'll have to!!!)

6

If you don't have a dream, how are you going to make a dream come true?

— *Oscar Hammerstein*

7

Are you known by the promises
you don't keep?

8

Have you noticed that 99% of
the things you worry about
don't ever happen?

Do you make decisions from a position of confidence or fear?

If you had to wear a T-shirt printed with a message of no more than eight words most accurately describing your outlook on life, what would your T-shirt say?

11

Are you a winner or a whiner?

12

If you don't know where you are going, how can you expect to get there?

Do you question your goals by asking, "Does this particular goal help me move toward my ultimate purpose in life?"

Are you making dust or eating dust?

— *Bill Grant*

Do you remember the things you were worrying about a year ago? How did they work out? Didn't you waste a lot of fruitless energy on account of most of them? Didn't most of them turn out to be all right after all?

— *Dale Carnegie*

How do you act when the pressure is on?

17

Are you on the path of something absolutely marvelous, or something absolutely mediocre?

18

Do you make promises or commitments?

Does failure discourage you or make you even more determined?

20

Are you already disappointed
with the future?

21

Which is bigger? How much
you do, or how much you get
done?

22

Is it a long way from your
words to your deeds?

Do you believe your doubts
and doubt your beliefs?

Have you been ignoring the still, small voice inside of you? What is it saying?

Do you judge each day not by the harvest, but by the seeds you plant?

How old is your attitude?

27

Are you making a cemetery out of your life by burying your talents and gifts?

28

Will people say this about your life: "He did nothing in particular, and he did it very well"?

What is your life mission? Is it written? Are you moving toward that life mission or away from it?

Has failure gone to your head?

31

If time and money were no problem, what would you dream?

32

Are you always ready to live, but never living?

What far-reaching effects could be set in motion by recognizing the purpose God has for your life and making a real commitment to begin to work toward that purpose today?

Ask yourself, "If I don't take action now, what will this ultimately cost me?"

Do you meet the problems and opportunities in your life with a decision?

Are you becoming ordinary?

37

Is your fear of loss much greater than your desire for gain?

38

Do you desire more than you can accomplish?

Does the path you're on capture your heart?

40

Do you think that you can lead
a successful sinful life?

41

Do you try to heal your hurts
or memorize them?

42

How much have the fears and
worries that never happened
cost you?

Are you deliberately planning to be less than you are capable of being?

44

If you had the power to do anything, how would you decide what to do?

45

How would you feel if you didn't accomplish your goals?

Are you willing to pay the price
of success?

If you could become famous for one thing in your life, what would it be?

48

If not you, then who? If not
now, then when?

— *Hillell*

49

Do you have a bright future?
Yes? No? Why?

Are you willing to give up what you have in order to become what you are not yet?

51

Are you thinking of security or opportunity?

What's the best use of your time right now?

Do you know where you are going?

Optimism is related to faith;
pessimism is related to doubt.
To which are you related?

Are you traveling, or are you going somewhere?

What's most important to you
in life?

57

What good is inspiration if it's not backed up with action?

58

What can you do to make yourself more valuable?

59

Do you think more about what you ought to do, or what you ought to be?

60

Would the boy you were be proud of the man you are?

Are you content with failure?

62

Does your reach exceed your grasp?

63

Did you know you're destined to be different?

64

Are you a fanatic?

What progress are you stand-ing in the way of?

— *Tim Redmond*

Where do you hear opportunity knocking? How can you answer that knock?

Take a look at your natural river. Where is your river going? Are you riding with it? Or are you rowing against it?

— *Carl Frederick*

Do you have opinions or convictions?

Do you try to start with what you have, or what you don't have?

What is one character trait you know you'd display no matter what circumstances you were facing?

71

Did you know that what you set your heart on determines how you spend your life?

72

Do you build a case against yourself?

Do you say, "I must do something," or do you say, "Something must be done"?

Are you a person of action or activity?

Do you still see yourself the way you were when you were age 15? 25? 35? 45? 55?

Do you say, "Let's find a way"
or "There is no way"?

77

Why don't you do what you know you should do?

78

What is one decision you would make if you knew it would not fail?

If you were to look your name up in the *World Book Encyclopedia,* what would it say?

If you're not you, then who
will you be?

81

Are you a "how" thinker or an "if" thinker?

82

When are you going to do something new and different?

83

What can you do to make better use of your time?

What impossible thing are you believing and planning for?

Do you say, "There should be a better way to do it," or "That's the way it's always been done"?

What is your most prevailing
thought?

87

What would a truly creative
person do in your situation?

88

Do you have a strong will or a
strong won't?

Have you found that the place to be happy is here, and the time to be happy is now?

Are you making a living or a life?

91

How would you complete this
sentence? "I am _____."

92

Do you rise early because no
day is long enough for a day's
work?

Who (what) are you becoming now?

94

If you aren't going all the way,
why go at all?

Forget your past. Who are you
now? Who have you decided
to become?

Are you trying to make some-thing *for* yourself or something *of* yourself?

97

After a failure or mistake, do you give up or get up?

98

Do you expect miracles?

Now that it's behind you, what did you do yesterday that you're proud of today?

100

Are you steering or drifting?

101

Do you demand more of yourself or excuse more of yourself?

102

Are you ice to truth and fire to falsehood?

Who of you by worrying can add a single hour to his life?

— *Jesus*

Looking
Outward

104

Which would you rather
have — a bouquet of flowers
or a packet of seeds?

— *Laurie Beth Jones*

105

Do you tackle problems bigger
than you?

"Who said it?" (An important question to ask of everything you believe.)

Are you motivated by what you really want out of life, or are you mass-motivated?

— *Earl Nightingale*

Is fear causing you to run from something that isn't after you?

Do you take time you would spend with a friend and give it to a critic?

110

Where else can you look for answers and ideas?

111

Both enthusiasm and pessimism are contagious. Which one do you spread?

If someone were to pay you ten dollars for every kind word you ever spoke and collect five dollars for every unkind word, would you be rich or poor?

What is the fruit on the
negative-thinkers' tree?

114

If revenge is sweet, why does it leave such a bitter taste?

115

Are you a creature of circumstance or a creator of circumstance?

Are you ready for your opportunity when it comes?

Do you leave others better
than you found them?

What would happen if you changed the words you spoke about your biggest problem? Your biggest opportunity?

Does adversity shatter or
shape your life?

120

Are you striking at the branches of your problems or at the root?

121

Are you spending your life trying to answer a question nobody's asking?

What is the value of the things you do most?

This is the test of your life:
How much is there left in you
after you have lost everything
outside of yourself?

— *Orison Marden*

Do you go where opportunity is or where opportunity is going?

Ten years from today, what will you wish you had done now?

Have you found that what you focus on determines how you feel?

What "opportunities" are currently before you (or what activities are you presently involved in) that might really be distractions?

If you were another person, would you like to be a friend of yourself?

Every once in a while ask yourself the question, "If money
weren't a consideration, what
would I like to be doing?"

130

When is the last time you did a
random act of kindness?

131

Do you see difficulties in every
opportunity, or opportunities
in every difficulty?

Do you go through a problem, or try to go around it and never get past it?

Do you make others feel bigger or smaller when they're around you?

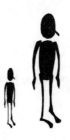

134

What could you accomplish if you were absolutely focused on what you want most in life?

135

What will you have to go through to get where you want to be?

Are you controlled by your thoughts, or are you controlling your thoughts?

— *Raymond Holliwell*

How can you get from here to wherever it is you want to be?

Do you look at the horizon and see an opportunity, or do you look into the distance and fear a problem?

Does something have to happen in order for you to feel good?

140

Do you focus on what you don't or what you do want to happen?

141

Whom do you usually blame when little or big things go wrong?

142

Are you too proud to ask for help?

143

If you try to be like him (or her), who will be like you?

How many people of great potential have you known? Where on earth did they all go?

Where should your focus be?

When confronted with a
Goliath-sized problem, which
way do you respond: "He's too
big to hit," or, like David,
"He's too big to miss"?

What walls are you building
right now?

148

What resources and solutions
are right in front of you?

149

Do you say, "I'm good, but not
as good as I ought to be," or
do you say, "I'm not as bad as
a lot of other people"?

Where do you hear opportunity knocking? How can you answer that knock?

What advice do you give others that you need to follow?

152

Do you ask more of yourself than others do?

153

Do you admit, "I was wrong," or do you say, "It wasn't my fault"?

When a problem strikes, do you ask, "Why me?" or "What can I learn from this?"

What one thing should you eliminate from your life because it holds you back from reaching your full potential?

Can others trust you?

Are you running *from* something or *to* something?

158

There's a force that shapes (dominates) your life. What is it?

159

What outside influences are causing you to be better or worse?

160

Whom do you need to forgive?

What good thing have you previously committed yourself to do that you have quit doing?

162

Who's creating your world?

163

How many people have you made homesick to know God?

What is one thing you can do for someone else who has no opportunity to repay you?

165

Do you make friends before
you need them?

If the future generations were dependent on you for spiritual knowledge, how much would they receive?

How many people do you know who became successful at something they hate?

168

If you were arrested for being kind, would there be enough evidence to convict you?

169

Why should people do business with you instead of your competitors?

What task do you most
frequently put off until
tomorrow that you should
do today?

Do your friends, family, and business associates increase your dreams or decrease your vision?

How many successful
complainers do you know?

Do you live by the Golden Rule today so you won't have to apologize for your actions tomorrow?

How many happy, selfish people do you know?

When it comes to doing things for others, are you one of those who will stop at nothing?

When confronted with an
obstacle, do you become
bitter or better?

177

Do you say, "If we can" or "How can we?"

178

Are you blending in or standing out?

Are you known as a solution
or a problem?

Do you jump at opportunities as quickly as you jump at conclusions?

181

What do you have to contribute
that will make a difference?

182

When things go wrong, do you
go with them?

Did you today, in any way, make the world a better place in which to live?

Are you keeping in step with the crowd or in step with yourself?

What are you really aiming at?

Are you more likely to have an important goal or to lack one?

187

Do you allow a past circumstance to limit today's happiness?

188

If not now, then when should you do it?

Do you do odd things to get even?

Do you anticipate trouble and worry about what may never happen?

Looking
Upward

Do you put a question mark
where God has put a period?

Do you spend the first six days
of each week sowing wild oats,
then go to church on Sunday
and pray for a crop failure?

—*Fred Allen*

Does God seem far away? If
so, guess who moved!

Do you say "Our Father" on Sunday and then act like an orphan the rest of the week?

In your prayers how often do you say, "And now, God, what can I do for You?"

Can you think of anything greater than knowing you are in the middle of God's will?

197

How regularly do you communicate with God?

198

Do you say: "Good morning, Lord!" or "Oh, no, Lord, it's morning"?

Are you putting out fires that God started?

Are you willing to do what God says (or what is right), even if it means standing alone?

201

Are you with Him or them?

202

Why worry when you can pray?

If you have God's promise for something, isn't that enough?

What is the first, small step
you can take to get moving?

Do you say thank you to God before you ask for something, or only after you get it?

How much of you does God have?

207

Did you know that God can give you hindsight in advance?

208

Hasn't God been good to you?

Do you have a passionate commitment to God's plan for your life?

Do you believe that you were destined to be doing what you are doing? Why or why not?

211

Are you thankful?

212

What do you believe in the depths of your being?

Who asks a king for a penny?
Why ask God only for
something trifling?

Did you know that what you believe is the force that determines what you attempt or fail to attempt to accomplish in your life?

Is the only time you do any deep praying when you find yourself in a hole?

Do you give up control of your life to something other than faith?

217

What cause are you living for?

218

When God tells you to do something, do you talk back?

219

The Lord is on my side; I will not fear: what can man do unto me? (Psalm 118:6)

220

How often do you ask God, "What are You up to today? Can I be a part of it?"

Do you see God everywhere or nowhere?

222

God has promised to be with you each step of the way (Joshua 1:9). What more can you ask for?

223

What puts meaning in your life?

What is between you and
God?

If God so arrays the grass of the field, which is alive today and tomorrow is thrown into the furnace, will He not much more do so for you, men of little faith?

— *Jesus*

What force is more powerful
than love?

Is God your hope or your excuse?

228

Do you risk enough to exercise your faith in God?

229

If everyone in the United States of America were on your level of spirituality, would there be a revival in the land?

Do you take things for granted
or with gratitude?

231

Are you willing to preach what you practice?

232

Do you reserve your best time for communion with God?

233

Is God finished with you yet?

234

Is there anything too hard for the Lord?

What is more miserable than being out of God's will?

What does God think about your future?

And if you hardhearted, sinful men know how to give good gifts to your children, won't your Father in Heaven even more certainly give good gifts to those who ask Him for them?

— *Jesus*

If Christ is the Way, why waste time traveling some other path?

239

How can the Lord guide you if you haven't made up your mind which way you really want to go?

240

The Lord is the strength of your life; of whom then shall you be afraid (Psalm 27:1)?

241

Are you waiting on God, or is He waiting on you?

242

Is Heaven only a complaint counter for you?

And how does a man benefit if he gains the whole world and loses his soul in the process?

— *Jesus*

When you die, why should God let you into Heaven?

Additional copies of
*Ask... (Life's Most Important Answers
Are Found in Asking the Right Questions)*
are available at fine bookstores
everywhere or directly from:

Insight International
P.O. Box 54996
Tulsa, OK 74155

Volume discounts available.

John Mason welcomes the opportunity to speak to your church, at conferences or retreats, or to men's, women's, and youth groups.

The following materials by John Mason are available from Insight International :

BOOKS:

An Enemy Called Average
You're Born an Original — Don't Die a Copy
Let Go of Whatever Makes You Stop
Words of Promise
*Don't Wait for Your Ship to Come In — Swim Out to
    Meet It*
Momentum Builders
*Ask... (Life's Most Important Answers Are
    Found in Asking the Right Questions)*

BOOKS-ON-TAPE:

"An Enemy Called Average"
"You're Born an Original — Don't Die a Copy"
"Let Go of Whatever Makes You Stop"

VIDEOS:

"Momentum: How To Get It, How To Have It,
    How To Keep It"
"Potential: There is Something Good Inside of You
    Waiting to Get Out"

About the Author

John Mason, best selling author and speaker, is on a mission to attack mediocrity. He speaks to the gifts and callings in people's lives, drawing out their greatest potential. He illuminates purpose and direction in others and gives them the Word to launch out.

He is the best selling author of: *An Enemy Called Average, You're Born an Original — Don't Die a Copy*, and *Let Go of Whatever Makes You Stop*. Each book is written and titled to fan the reader's potential into a blaze!

John is a popular and nationally recognized speaker at churches, conventions, and retreats.

Radio is also one of John's avenues for sharing this message. His captivating radio show called "Wait-A-Minute" is aired daily on over 400 stations across the United States. This show is based on short excerpts from his books. Listeners have been changed by these bite-size truths for daily living.

Foremost, he is a remarkable husband and father. John, his wife Linda, and their four children: Michelle, Greg, Michael, and David reside in Tulsa, Oklahoma.